Eternal Conversations

Reflections
and
Illuminations
for Higher Existence

Damon McGregor

Copyright © 2017
Library of Congress

Cover art by my Father,

Jock McGregor

jockmcgregorart.com

This set of quotes are originals produced by myself at different times of my life, starting off in my first year as an undergraduate. I realize that almost nothing is original, since everything has been said at least once by somebody, somewhere. But these are my attempts at creations of realization that are, or were, at least at the time, new to me. I intend to re-examine and extend each illumination over time, and to incorporate each into future paragraphs, chapters, or complete books.

Thank You Very Much

Only an Occasional Resting Point

The years become minutes,
The minutes, years.
Old age comes from behind,
And then into sight.
Praising, and damning you,
For what you did and did not.
But you thank him
For the laughter and tears,
And for the opportunity to have been there,
And to be here,
And to be
Apart of this inexorable journey,
With no destination in particular,
Never having had a destination in
Particular to begin with,

Only an occasional resting point.

Live as though you are already an old man looking back.

~~~

It is best to live one's life as though it is on a time-line. The past should be remembered for historical reasons, the present should be paid attention to, and the future should be envisioned for as best as possible. Cornerstones and monuments should be placed into time-line slots to secure particular parts of history to oneself. This way one will be able to look back on these cornerstones and monuments when he or she is old, since these will stand out and be remembered most, and in that way one can be proud with integrity instead of despair at what one has done with his or her's own life. This is how one lives as though he is already an old man looking back.

~~~

One should not live one's entire life in the complete anticipation of being old, because youth does not last long, and it can never be completely regained. The old man self should simply be remained aware of.

~~~

Pay attention to existence. This is the first step in growing old with integrity: paying attention to a vanishing existence along the way of your life.

~~~

Pay attention to the vanishing moments, like the ways of life that have vanished before. Existence is ephemeral.

~~~

One must pay attention to others in case he only becomes a simple 'brick in the wall'.

~~~

Paying attention to surroundings and work, thinking for work, thinking for oneself, paying attention to loved ones and work, and thinking about loved ones and work all simultaneously is very trying and seemingly paradoxical. One could choose to focus on one and not the others, but in doing so would lose out on experiencing a huge chunk of living, as many typically do, staying engaged in the same mode of focus of only one or the other, usually work, themselves, or surroundings. In this way most of the rest of life is missed.

~~~

Focusing too much or too little can lead one into the abyss.

~~~

Focusing too much or too little about what others think can lead one into trouble, can cause one to go nowhere.

~~~

Living life as a routine entails the danger of coming to the end of it realizing that one has never stopped to 'look around'. One should simply be aware of his or her surroundings and enjoy what spontaneity can bring.

~~~

Trying to line-up or schedule errands and tasks does not always work, sometimes tasks just have to do be done out of order, because if any of them cannot happen during a certain period of time, then one may be waiting a long time, if ever, to get them all done. This is mainly for the obsessive-compulsive, schedule-oriented—many of them stay miserable most of their lives wishing things had gone according to schedule.

~~~

It is the destruction of *ideals* that cause people to become bitter and resent life and the world. Many people accept or create ideals when they are a kid— from the media, their parents, religion, culture, etc.— when these ideals are not met, part of that person's fiber is destroyed. It doesn't have to be that way though, all you have to do is re-evaluate what the media, religion, culture, etc. have to tell you about what is 'ideal' or 'sacred', then adapt; or you can simply not give up and try again even harder and wiser if you strongly want that ideal to match your interests and personality.

~~~

When you feel like doing something, hurry-up and do it while the feeling still lasts, or risk the feeling being lost forever. Not in the case of making careless decisions, but in deeds such as showing a best friend appreciation, or telling your Dad that you love him.

~~~

Born to die! But live for LIFE, while you still can!...

~~~

Feel the now!
One is only *ultimately* alive if one is in the moment. In this I am not professing selfishness. Just because one must live one's life for oneself in the moment, does not mean that others are not involved. By making others around who are involved in one's life happy, one will become happier in return, as he or she is enlightened by the environment, and by setting the stage for more 'entertainment' of various sorts.

~~~

One's entire life should not be lived internally, such as by only reading about mountains or beaches. The rocks of the mountains should actually be felt, and the sand should thoroughly be felt between the toes.

~~~

Ambition is only a good starting place. The rest is up to reason and careful planning in order to execute.

~~~

If being the best is what is desired, and if someone is not being the best at what he or she is doing, then that person is forgoing time at being the best at something else.

~~~

At some point, one should do permanent things, things which can be placed on one's tombstone. This will make a person less nervous on a day to day basis and will make that person feel more secure and comfortable with him or herself inside. Examples are obtaining a Master's degree, writing a book, making a song, or a great work of art.

~~~

Things can <u>always</u> get worse.

~~~

Pessimists refuse to be naïve.

~~~

Optimists refuse to lose.

~~~

Only those who are weak fail to allow optimism to succeed in their lives. Life is too short to live it so negatively, this will only lead to destructive thought instead of constructive thought. Pessimism keeps one from being naïve, but a simple awareness of the "dark side" can be attained in order to keep one from harms. The formula could be 10-30% pessimism, and 70-90% optimism. This would aid in thought of the highest levels—pure thought—without the weights or inhibitions of pessimism.

~~~

I need to realize how amazing other people are so I can become amazing with them.

~~~

Growing-up is the increasing realization of how much one's actions affect others, and is also the increasing realization of the actuality of mortality.

~~~

One should always do what is timeless.

~~~

The years will become minutes, while the years will still leave their marks.

~~~

If the time is not questioned, no clocks, then time goes unnoticed.

~~~

Living in 'the present' is paradoxically both the toughest and the easiest state to live in.

~~~

Some days, more can be done in an hour than in a day. Sometimes whole days are spent trying to do one hour.

~~~

Go from reality to dreams, and from dreams to reality....

~~~

Wisdom takes maintenance. Existence, including knowledge and learnt material, is in a constant state of flux, is ever changing and evolving according to particular points in history, and so one can never think that he or she has gained wisdom and then stop there. Wisdom must be remembered, updated, thrown out if necessary, or replaced. Even though some wisdom seems timeless, it can still not apply or be befitting to certain circumstances or periods of time. Wisdom acquired though time must be maintained.

~~~

Starting to avoid mirrors is a bad sign. If one no longer wants to look at oneself, then there is something that he or she is avoiding, something that needs to be fixed in order to allow him or her to stand up tall and look themselves straight in the eye.

~~~

Create a simple life from a complex mind.

~~~

Fashion everything in life as a garden. Plant a good seed in rich soil, add fertilizer, water it everyday, provide sunlight, prune it, and lastly add support.

~~~

Feel the cold, feel the heat. Do not always shelter yourself into a state of equilibrium. Go outside sometimes when it is freezing cold, suffer every once and awhile from the August heat. Remind yourself once again that you are human and alive. *Moments of suffering are memorable.*

~~~

Magic is simply anything that we do not understand.

~~~

See through the eyes of a child, and world becomes magical again.

~~~

Magic is still real. The systems and connections observed in scientific reasoning simply show the mechanisms of magic, or how the magic works. It does not prove that magic does not exist. We still cannot escape or fully understand how the physical laws are, or came to be, like time, motion, space, and the will. *How we saw the world as a child still remains.*

~~~

Beware of what sells the most.

~~~

The old fear that the young will about them.

~~~

There is no other time to hang out, youth is wasting, phases change, people get older quickly and move on. Use it or loose it, now or never. Don't wait years to hang out, or miss the boat.

~~~

Phases are not only for the young, never stop going through them in order to learn as many aspects of humanity as one possibly can do in a short lifetime.

~~~

I carry the people in my past like assimilated ghosts—alter-egos which comprise the multiplicity of myself.

~~~

It gets tough keeping up with the selves one acquires or expresses over time.

~~~

As people get older, they desperately search for those who are fit enough to carry them to the grave. What I mean by this, is that people want to have those around them, or make friends with those who will remember them, you are younger and more fit to carry his or her ideas and ideals on in order to establish a link to immortalization.

~~~

It is best to let older people pour out their wisdom, not one of them, but all of them, whether good or bad. Then sift and reap.

~~~

Many younger people do not realize where older people have been in the past. They do not realize that the older person they are today, may not even be close to the person they were in the past. Many people take on different hats and shoes throughout a lifetime. Many younger people can only see the appearance of who someone looks like they are today. For example, a parent may have once been "hot" and "cool", but now they may be "rule-following" and "responsible", this occurs because of gaining years of long-sightedness. A person may not even resemble the person they once were. Another example is that a young person now sees the slower, older man, but that man may be slow today because he was once been the fastest, hardest working person alive, and so wore his body out and down to its current state. Through age, children will acquire longsightedness and retrospection in order to see and understand how people go through phases and changes, how someone cannot even be recognizable at different points in life. But children and even adults should try hard to understand that people go through phases, because it is important for understanding and tolerance, for compassion, to allow themselves and others to grow and evolve into higher beings.

~~~

The older we get, we tend to physically move around less, but become more sensitive to the nuances that accompany the actions in life. The realization of these nuances is acquired mostly through trial-and-error over the years and decades, and by reflection of the actions which accompanied these trial-and-error experiences. *If we choose to accept it, the world can become richer and fuller, making us wiser and giving us goggles which can allow us to see more and more aesthetically.*

~~~

Youth can be threatening to older people.

~~~

As people get older, sadly enough, many replace sex with food, thus decline in health.

~~~

As people get older, they forget the will, strength, emotions, and flexibility of the younger body, and how and why the youth can do and act as they do. Having kids is the best reminder.

~~~

As people get older, they tend to act like their parents, because they want to experience how and why their parents raised them the way that they did. It is important for most to experience the circumstances and emotions that undertook their parents while raising them, so that they can get a better perspective on themselves: to get a better grip on how and why they are the way that they are.

~~~

Many are programmed over time believing that they are supposed to act a certain way at a certain age. Never grow up. "Don't grow up, it's a trap!" Ceasing 'playing' makes one grow old. Responsibility can be maintained or increased with age, no problem. It is important to remain with childhood eyes.

~~~

Never regret the past—simply see it as a chapter of life from which to learn what, or what not to do, next, or later in life.

~~~

It is a great feeling to increasingly be able to look down upon the things that were once to looked up to.

~~~

We are all going to die.
Many people mess up their wholes lives because they
do not realize this simple fact. They may become
aware of this when they are old and it is too late,
thus being in despair that they are going to die
without ever having 'lived'.

~~~

It is best to live with, and befriend 'slaves' in order to learn the obvious factors of confinement first (such as appearances and circular reasoning), then one can move on to more unobvious factors (such as those that are involved with government, custom, politics, etc.) Then, higher realms of thinking can be given ground to begin, such as metaphysics, existentialism, and spirituality.

~~~

It is never either/or, but all or none, and then some.

~~~

The feeling of being young is the feeling that the world is a wide open place of opportunity for growth and accomplishment. That is the essence of the early twenties. Most people kill this feeling off in their mid to late twenties. Full force adaptability and a constant learning environment should stay in place to remain in a sense "forever young".

~~~

What a difference 20 years can make in a human life: such as from birth to the age of 20, from 20 to 40, 40 to 60, 60 to 80, and 80 to 100. The differences between the stages are very deep and wide.
Each decade is also a phenomenal leap. Even 5 years can put gray hair and wrinkles on some people.

~~~

Learning is the fountain of youth.
Ceasing to learn makes one grow old quickly.

~~~

Ceasing to learn anything new will eventually make one miserable.

~~~

My philosophy on learning is that just one concept, sentence, or even just one single word, can change your perspective of yourself and the world around you completely and forever. How many of these perspectives await!?

~~~

Freeing someone's mind frees one's own as well.

~~~

What every person or pet enjoys the most is being paid attention to.
What every person loves the most is to not be forgotten.

~~~

Most human interactions are reciprocal.

~~~

Typically, people with nice faces take advantage of others. Everyone stares and gazes into his or her eyes, allowing room for gravitational pull, deceit, or dominance. This taking advantage of does not have to be deceitful always, but can be used to influence others with a simple stare, a gaze into beauty, a "drawing in" to fulfill wishes.

~~~

What is philosophy good for? Well, it teaches one not *what* to think, but *how* to think.

~~~

Philosophy is not a luxury in itself, but is a necessity in order to obtain luxury of various forms of wealth.

~~~

What lies between the disciplines of knowledge is poetry. It is the glue which binds Philosophy, Biology, Psychology, English, Mathematics, and all the rest of the disciplines together into one.

~~~

Existentialism is like a breeze of wind that is experienced over and over again throughout a lifetime. No beginning, middle, or end.

~~~

The best philosophy is symmetrical in nature. The same can be said for beauty.

~~~

Being one with nature should not be an aim, but a given, an already is, no different from time and space.

~~~

The main difference between men and women is that men typically have stronger muscles and women can get pregnant: everything else follows from this.

~~~

Women tend to make sudden dramatic changes to their personality and lifestyle, especially after Motherhood. Whereas men tend to stay relatively the same throughout the lives.

~~~

Bitterness is contagious.

~~~

Misery is tempting

~~~

Never underestimate the importance of waiting a long time to make big decisions. Never do anything that will yield long-term psychological negative consequences. One decision can impact one for the entirety of his or her life. Examples are cheating on a spouse, taking a certain highly addictive drug, or betraying a friend.

~~~

Those that shackle themselves hate free spirits.

~~~

One receives great opposition from those who are not on the path of fulfilling their own existences.

~~~

Appetites cannot be reasoned in retrospect.

~~~

When there is a choice, take the scenic route.

~~~

Naivety perceives more naivety than not.

~~~

"It depends on how you look at it," could be the truest statement of all for human beings.

~~~

Stop stressing; one can only go so fast.

~~~

One strong reason for not being able to sleep at night means that ideals are not being met.

~~~

If one thinks that he has to master it from the beginning, then he or she will most often not even begin.

~~~

The rules must be learned first, in order to more efficiently and effectively break them. Learn by the rules to beat them at their own game.

~~~

Some want fixed rules and states, some want flux or dependence upon specific causes.

~~~

Language, statistics, science, in fact, our entire body of knowledge, are the same regarding truth. They are simply the best we can do.

~~~

The strongest reason for reading is that life is too short for only trial-and-error.

~~~

When you have reading material, you will never wait in line again.

~~~

Being cynical does not equal being intellectual .

~~~

Every experience can be a learning experience if applied creatively.

~~~

Existential self-awareness has been rapidly increasing since the advent of digital cameras, cell phone cameras, cell phone camcorders, basically, the rise of cheaper and cheaper means of photographing and filming. A person can literally take a picture of, and film him or herself every single day. The reason why this increases self-awareness is because that person can look back on themselves years from now and become aware of every 'step' that person took in order to get themselves where they are in comparison to where they came from—comparisons of increases in intelligence and maturity in particular. Before these inventions, say in the 1800's and before, some people had nothing but a mirror, nothing to rely on but memory in how they appeared and acted, seeing themselves only from a subjective point of view. It is now far easier to view and understand oneself objectively.

~~~

It seems as though because of the lust for shock value, the news now reports worse information and occurrences because of the introduction of cameras, camcorders, and the internet on cell phones. In this way, much more news can be reported, so the media can now pick and choose the worst news to show for the sake of ratings. More information, more 'cherry-picking'.

~~~

We are all going to die,
And that is one of the greatest realizations that one
can ever have, so that we can live before we die.

~~~

The greatest measures should be taken to ensure
that one could die happily and peacefully at any
moment.

~~~

Yourself is the only person that you can never
escape. That is why you should pay attention to and
listen to yourself at all costs so that you can at least
be your own friend, and you will then always have
good company with decent conversation material.

~~~

Revenge is unnecessary. Those who purposely injure
others will destroy themselves from the inside out
over time with bitterness and self-hatred. No action
needs to be taken. In this way more conflict can be
avoided.

~~~

Designing the most beautiful life possible is the greatest art form.

~~~

Whoever makes A's can be whomever they want.

~~~

Looking at the table of contents is better than nothing.
A surprising amount of information on subjects can be gained by mentally filling in between the chapter titles by what one already knows. Though this can be dangerous, once again it is still better than nothing.

~~~

The intelligence of someone cannot be determined simply by the way that he or she talks.

~~~

Judgment is either hit or miss, depending on the mind, the time, or the circumstance.

~~~

One should aspire to fashion one's mind as a fine diamond: clear and symmetrical.

~~~

What happens to the pretty girls when they have kids and do not have the hours to be pretty anymore? This is a good reason to develop a mind.

~~~

Most people are not stupid, just simply undeveloped.

~~~

Desire is the enemy of intellect.

~~~

A constant state of naivety persistently persists.

~~~

All knowledge is based on belief.

~~~

Irrationality easily multiplies when under the impression of ingenuine or impulsive emotions.

~~~

Unfinished past memories resurface and resonate when the mind is under-stimulated.

~~~

When manual labor is done all day, there is a yearn for mental work, and when mental work is done all day, there is a yearn for physical labor. This must be taken into consideration when wishing for the other side of the grass, and for realizing that both must be done in order to be a balanced person.

~~~

One can never think that he or she is the most intelligent, because every creature has a different perception of reality, therefore a different set of intelligence. Wasps or fish are examples.

~~~

The most difficult challenge is to change *one's own* beliefs.

~~~

The benefit of the doubt should be given to everyone. Many surprises await!

~~~

The best way to fight for freedom is to read the most hardcore books one can possibly find.

~~~

Look no further. Heaven and Hell exist right here on Earth.

~~~

Life is my playground.

~~~

Simply starting to tinker around is how one begins doing anything that requires some level of mastery. Perfection cannot not be attained from the beginning.

~~~

Neuroticism is the result of over-extending and non-production.

~~~

When people talk bad about someone in front of someone else, that person is either talking bad about the person they are speaking to behind their backs also, or it is because that person does not talk bad about the person he or she is speaking to behind their backs, because of the fact that they are confiding in them.

~~~

Sometimes kids destroy things to see how they were put together.

~~~

It is best to live in the past, present, and future simultaneously to utmost one's existence. Remember the past to provide yourself with learning tools, live in the present since that is all that actually exists, and be aware of a future and a self that you aspire to create. By doing this, by keeping all three in mind simultaneously, one can live fully.

~~~

Being too busy is a very poor excuse when it comes to caring for others. It typically has a very poor reception.

~~~

Controlling/manipulative people have certain mechanics: they are nice to people until they are just a bit too far in, and then they strike and subdue (scream at someone or whatever). But many times by then, one is too well invested to get out. This develops into a mechanism, which is rotating between being nice and screaming (or worse). This mechanism is effective because the controlling person knows that if all they do is scream, most people will reach a breaking point and get out, but if they are really nice to you in between abuses (fake smiles and gifts), it creates a balance that keeps many lingering around long enough to take the abuse.

~~~

Time must be taken control of, in order for it to not be controlling. Prioritizing needs and goals is the only way.

~~~

Marry your friend, and whoever will be a good Mother or Father to your children.

~~~

Insecurity breeds righteousness.

~~~

Some people are only happy or nice when they are agreed with.

~~~

Life is too short to be *overly* concerned with details.

~~~

When someone is *really* going to do something grand, it is not spoken of, not a word, it is just done.

~~~

Though seemingly obvious, sitting around and waiting for one to do something with one's life does not work. It has to be discovered while doing something else. Thinking while working. At least something will be accomplished in the mean time. Doing one thing leads to the thoughts of doing other things.

~~~

Presume every kid is a genius, it cannot hurt and can only help.

~~~

It is strange that once a certain mood is projected towards somebody during the first few encounters of meeting that person, then it is often very hard to break out of that certain 'mood' during the next few encounters with that same person, even if that mood is ingenuine, inappropriate, and has nothing to do with the person.

~~~

Being normal is the easier route.

~~~

There are very few 'normal' people when lives are more closely inspected.

~~~

Creativity comes in all forms and subjects, including both English and Math.

~~~

One is not attracted to someone or something on purpose.

~~~

Doing something for a long enough period of time tends to define a person.

~~~

People seem to have acquired a need to be punished for their wrongdoings. If they are not punished by any outside source, they will most likely punish themselves in some form.

~~~

It is easier to be 'evil' and irresponsible.

~~~

Someone is addicted to something when he or she cannot think normally without it.

~~~

There is a huge difference between being concerned and worrying. Being concerned involves reason and logic, whereas worrying does not.

~~~

Some people worry or stay angry all the time just to give themselves something to do.
In these cases time should be filled more productively, more creatively.

~~~

**Resisting life and difficulty is what makes life hard.
Do not resist.**

~~~

This is how I would live to be a hundred years old:
I would refrain from excessive habits, I would
exercise regularly, mostly cardiovascular types of
exercise, and some lifting of weights. I would eat
more fish and vegetables instead of red meat and
snacks. I would make sure that I use every muscle in
my body to keep the muscles from deteriorating
from the lack of use, because the pains and
weaknesses of body parts through aging are simply a
result of a lack of their use. I would have regular
check-ups with a doctor every few months, and I
would check every part of my body for any sign of
deterioration. I would stay mentally active by
continuously reading books (Philosophy and Logic)
and magazines (Discover and Men's Health) simply to
stay apart of the cutting edge. I would continue to
practice logical skills to prevent the loss of
cognition—no calculators! I would learn to love as
much as possible and be self-less to ensure that
others are there to keep me in social realms.

~~~

Specializing is a form of mental suicide. For some the only pieces of their mind left are the parts which contain the subject they specialized in. All other parts have been diminished, narrowed down, biased, or erased. The mind should never be narrowed but expanded.

~~~

It is perfectly OK to take risks, as long as all future options, outcomes, and consequences are thoroughly calculated and weighed in order to make progress.

~~~

Fear is the greatest distortion of all.

~~~

Balance is the key to life, *but balance must be maintained.* A state of balance cannot be reached and then expected to stay in one place.

~~~

One of the difficulties in life is trying to maintain a state of balance and homeostasis. For instance, people in their early 20s may find a way of living which suites them best, various routines and what not. They may think that they have found the perfect way for them to live, only to have that way interrupted, for example, by jobs, kids, house, wife/husband, etc. Then they must find a new way to balance or allow for homeostasis for themselves, a way in which they feel like they can be most comfortable. This interruption occurs over and over and over again throughout life. Change is inevitable. All we can do is adapt or be miserable.

~~~

It is better to gain wisdom *before* one is old. Most wish they had done things differently. All older people have hang-ups. We all will have some sort of hang-ups, but we can reduce them by reading and trying to experience as much as possible, all of the ups and downs, as quickly as possible in order to reduce them, to live as though we are already old looking back.

~~~

Doing actions *in increments*, instead of all at one time, as in the case of learning and exercise, will increase chances of success. This seems obvious, but many try to jump to the end result, and so fail to get past the beginning.

~~~

One has to find out what is good about oneself
before one can take control of his or her life, and
then be freed of the chains of bitterness and
unhappiness. One has to have a place to start....what
one is good at, what does he or she value, how are
those goods and values beneficial to oneself, loved
ones, society, and life in general?

~~~

Intimate relationships consist of three parts: Lust,
Love, and Logic. Some consist of one more than the
other, but a well-balanced relationship is in unity of
all three equally.

~~~

Children and teens are channeled into roles and paths that are being provided in a template form by the media, where as they usually have no other substitutes that are as glorified and exalted. Powerful influences are exerted on the minds of children and adolescents as they are exploited for the pure purpose of monetary gain. Profit is what rules in this business-oriented society, and America has stepped to new lows in first attacking the adolescents, and now taking cheap shots at children to get them started on the same path in feeding the economic giants. Using sex for shopping, money for personal value, aggression for problem-solving, and achievement for worthiness by undermining children and adolescents because of their consumer determinism, is a major factor in the destruction of character in America's tomorrow. Inexperienced, impressionable minds that are creating new pathways into self-discovery, are being misinformed and mislead by the American media, which is casting molds for "clay" youth to step inside.

~~~

Better to live in a shack, and be imbued with education that has infinite value (such as philosophy), than in a mansion and have little internal mental value.

~~~

Nature is intelligent.

~~~

One of the best parts about being a child is having no concept of time.

~~~

There are millions of ways to view the world, but some do seem better than others. It takes an equal balance of what 'actually' happened or what is 'actually' 'going on' to get to the truth better—there are positive aspects of certain life situations, just are there are negative.

~~~

Everyone has something to say, but that doesn't mean that every person should be listened to, simply considered.

~~~

Responsibility needs to be taken for one's own actions. Excuses for failure need to cease. It is easier to blame the world. Full freedom must be exercised with what one has to work with. Determinates do exist, but only the weak let them win. By this way, natural de-selection can be avoided.

~~~

Imagine taking all the negative energy, and converting that same energy into positive energy. Imagine what could then be accomplished. That same energy has the power to either accomplish great deeds, or destroy.

~~~

Letting go of hang-ups and feuds becomes more important as we get older. More time and energy should be spent elsewhere, such as on family and careers in order to get somewhere in life. Many people hold grudges their whole lives, wasting time and energy becoming bitter and hung-up.

~~~

One must be willing to SACRIFICE some aspects of life for others if he or she wants it bad enough, he must be willing to sacrifice pieces of his life to build other parts. It all depends on what is most important to him at that particular time—family, friends, school, work, money, publishing, physical activities—some will have to be sacrificed more for others. This can be accomplished by an arrangement of a personal hierarchy of needs.

~~~

Truth must be told at the right time. There are very narrow spaces in which truth must be interjected, when someone is open. Often that space opens for a moment, and then closes back into automatic mode. If a truth must be told, then don't miss the chance, say it when that space is open, or possibly miss the opportunity forever.

~~~

We will never get out of here alive, but we can at least increase our odds.

~~~

The best advice, is to follow your own first.

~~~

Before radio and television, there was imagination.

~~~

Reading is better than television—the pictures are better.

~~~

Mental or physical labor can be equally tiring.

~~~

Contemporarily there are so much external stimuli from the media, that there isn't much room for internal stimuli anymore.

~~~

Mathematics can give one a gambler's high: playing the cards of what one's got to produce results that win or lose. It is the challenge of this win or lose scenario that keeps one playing the Mathematics game of various forms.

~~~

What many people miss about addiction is the addiction itself. That is, the excitement of the want/need relationship involved in addiction. One is never alone when addiction is present with the addict. The addict in this way always has someone or something to connect with, or to.

~~~

Money - it simply comes and goes, making it unimportant in comparison to things which are lasting, such as wealth or trophies of different forms.

~~~

It is impossible to be creative without the sight of intuition.

~~~

Those who are time crunchers receive the most respect from society.

~~~

Society will not let you do whatever you want to do.

~~~

"Stupidity" can simply be a side-effect from not getting enough nutrition. Proper nourishment is imperative to proper brain function, therefore well-being.

~~~

There is a great difference between being smart and being wise. Being smart involves knowing facts and primarily being able to compute complex information. Being wise involves knowing the difference between fact and fiction, between knowledge and reality, and between the conceptual and the aconceptual.

~~~

There is nothing wrong with 'compensation' in most cases. It is simply someone trying to create balance in his or her life. Good examples are someone who builds a perfect body to compensate for not having done well in school, or someone who builds a perfect brain to compensate for not being attractive. It is an attempt at balance. But compensation can also be used in the wrong way—such as someone having sex with many people to compensate for the love that they did not get from their parents, or someone relying on materialistic objects such as money or possessions to compensate for *an internal self that was never developed*. So there is nothing wrong with compensation as a practice, but beware that there can be a dark side. Allow the light to bring one's faults or shortcomings from the bottom of the pit, to the top of the pyramid, Olympics style. It is an attempt at symmetry.

~~~

There is nothing wrong with contrast.

~~~

There is a thin line between sex and murder.

~~~

Dress like a lawyer, get away with murder. Most do not suspect the guy in the suit and tie. Trust the guy in a tank top and flip flops, not the guy in a suit and tie.

~~~

Some people use extreme chronic happiness as a strong defense mechanism for chronic stress and sadness.

~~~

Worrying too much about what others think will get one nowhere.

~~~

Fire is a living thing: it breathes, it eats or consumes, it wastes, it multiplies or grows, and seemingly desires.

~~~

Friends should not have to have reasons to call or stop by.

~~~

Some people are only happy when they are agreed with or "cheer-leaded".

~~~

I would prefer to be a writer than a scholar. The difference is that a writer writes his own and makes his own way, whereas a scholar writes about what someone else already wrote.

~~~

When the issue is looked upon deep enough, any conservative becomes a liberal, or any liberal becomes a conservative.

~~~

Hollywood's celebrities are the new genre of Greek gods—they are worshipped, followed, and displayed or suggested to the world how people are, or are not supposed to act.

~~~

It is easier to deconstruct than it is to construct.

~~~

One cannot fix a mind or body when one does not even know what is broken in the first place.

~~~

There is never one single 'mold' in which a particular category can be placed, such as 'cute', but there are instead quantities and variations of. Realizing this is a cornerstone of growing-up.

~~~

It is not easy for *anyone* to be thyself.

~~~

There are two ways to stay mentally healthy: deal with problems right away, and do not repress problems. Undealt with and repressed problems will manifest themselves in various unconscious ways such as neurosis or nervousness, which in turn always needs a cure of some sort (drugs, alcohol, "medicine", or [even more depression, which ironically is used as comforter itself)].

~~~

For every bad day (considering there is not a chronic illness), the next day is usually always a good day. This mechanism seems to be a filtering of life's frustrations: a filtering of negative emotions which bring light into brand new days. This is well to be remembered during a terrible day.

The older one gets—having more experience to draw on—the more one is able to realize these cycles, and is more aware that if one waits, then eventually life will become new again. Failing to recognize these cycles is major reason why many teenagers commit suicide, they haven't lived long enough to realize that if they just wait it out, then their conditions will eventually improve, that that person that they broke up with is not the all and end all, for example. The end of the world and one's life does not come in every slump one falls into. Just wait it out and with a little effort and support from fellow human beings, life is will improve and often be much better than it was before. This takes time to realize. This is one of the best benefits of experience.

~~~

The deepest level of the criminal mind is suicidal. Those who are willing to murder often care less whether or not they die themselves. The same could go for heavy drug use, often people would rather do coke or heroin in place of killing themselves though they wish to die, thus the risk becomes nothing; that is the reason why people make those type of choices, and is the reason why people who are not suicidal cannot understand why these people make them in the first place.

~~~

Drinking can be a slippery slope.

~~~

Selfish people can envelope their lives around themselves by say, drinking, then spending a lot of time hung-over, then working, then resting, then drinking, then being occupied with being sick and hung-over, etc., etc. This way they will never have time for others.

~~~

Pathology causes pathology, depression adds gravity to itself, anxiety feeds on itself to multiply, and self-doubt/self-defeating behavior adds gasoline to its own flame. The opposite direction must be pulled with the will as soon as a grip can be taken on a stable enough "surface".

~~~

Fear can breed from not knowing what one is doing at all. But then, once certain goals have been accomplished, one thinks they have been champ all along. The fear is forgotten in an instant, and 'the champ' acts as if fear had never been there all along. It is too quickly forgotten. Many adults forget this when dealing with children and teens, because children and teens often experience fear and anxiety when faced with brand new challenges, ones that adults have already faced, dealt with, and been through, but then the adults have forgotten the fear as soon as it has passed, and so often do not understand or relate to the newborn fears of the young.

~~~

This is how mastery motivation, learned helplessness, learning goals, and performance goals are related: Learned helplessness is a tendency to avoid challenges and a perception that there is little to be done to improve, that external forces are keeping one from achieving and not from a lack of effort. Learned helplessness is related to performance goals because with performance goals, oneself is not adaptable to the environment, instead they are in a fixed state of ability. They are essentially closely related because both terms refer to a fixed state of ability and not on effort of the individual. It is not how hard they try, it is what the environment plans to do with them. Learning goals are the perception of the individual that ability is a changeable, adaptable trait that is influenced by effort and not by the environment. This is closely related to mastery orientation in that both terms refer to a perception of the ability to master the environment through hard work and dedication, it is the people who have this attitude that become not just good but great.

~~~

People often commit the fallacy of treating people how they expect they will be treated. The people being treated in such a way often act how others expect that they will act as well.

~~~

I know...I don't know.

~~~

What I don't know, I know, and what I know, I don't know.

~~~

A mind is constantly lost, only to be constantly found.

During that lost process, learning and understanding takes place. The finding is touching base again.

~~~

It is better to live in a world of "reality" as opposed to a world of fiction, because "reality" is more difficult, and so must be put up to the challenge in order to utmost existence by taking the harder, richer route. More experience can be gained in this way.

~~~

One of the greatest things to be learned is just how *different*, different people's minds are; and how completely OK that is.

~~~

The ultimate education in philosophy is hanging around with as many different types of people as possible.

~~~

The ultimate form of education is traveling.

~~~

Being bored is one's own fault.

~~~

Boredom feels like dying.

~~~

In many cases it is not what one does, it is what one does not do.

~~~

Temporarily suppressing traits tends to strengthen them.

~~~

I do not want life to pass me by, I want me to pass by life.

~~~

Some people do not want to write down their recipes. They find it disruptive to the hand-me-downs and oral traditions, which to many have much higher value.

~~~

Between the different art forms, none are objectively better than the other, one is simply different from the next.

~~~

Having the ability to do something, and not doing it, is what makes one bitter. But, just because one has the ability to do something, does not mean that they actually *want* to do it. Being forced in this way can cause bitterness as well, having the opposite effect.

~~~

Judging from the make-up and physics of the universe, it could simply be an atom or a molecule, possibly of a larger piece of matter.

~~~

It is of the utmost importance to be comfortable in one's own body. This is primarily acquired by liberal arts education, exercise, and properly dealing with one's 'demons'.

~~~

Live as both King and Peasant.

~~~

The more I learn, the less I seem to know.

~~~

In life, everything contains its opposites: behaviors, thoughts, emotions, actions, etc. One action will indefinitely and eventually lead to its opposite, especially extreme actions. So one must be careful when considering what opposite implication will instantly or eventually be applied when making decisions or choosing to feel certain ways.

~~~

Emotions cannot be hidden behind glossed over eyes, or "popped out" veins.

~~~

When someone calls someone "sick" in making a statement about themselves or someone else, that action reveals that something deep and true has been tapped. There would not be such an extreme reaction if what was said did not affect that person in a way which meant something deep and true, if not, then there would be no reaction worth mentioning.

~~~

Death, garbage, and feces are all inappropriate and not to be spoken of, but reflect a large majority of the truest nature of our human reality.

~~~

One truly is, what one does not know one is, it is what others see.

~~~

"Well,....it depends"....Something always depends on the former or the next. There are no isolated statements or pieces of thought.

~~~

Complete satisfaction is impossible, so we may as well be content with what it is near.

~~~

It is not a mental illness if it is controllable. It is instead the embodiment of creativity and imagination that has become boundless.

~~~

Distractions keep you from doing your best work.

Personal definitions:

Good - advantageous to the progress of life.

Evil - inhibiting or disabling to the progress of life.

Reality - a personal network of perceptions comprised of past, present, and potential memories. Reality is also a subjective experience of an objective reality, whatever that objective reality may be.

Normal - what is expected.

Wisdom – knowledge that can be used to better the world and lives of oneself *and* others, not just knowledge that is acquired and retained for the sake of knowing—this I call *dead knowledge*, not wisdom.

Thinking – a process of taking information obtained from the outside world and constructing it into structures that the mind uses to adapt, maintain, and utmost one's existence in the world that surrounds him or her. It is a tool that allows some to survive better that others.

Creativity - taking a small amount of information, and multiplying that same amount of information exponentially.

Reading - the activity of producing visuals and feelings through means of the eye or hand being read or felt, usually on paper.

~~~

My -er theory:

Everyone and everything can still be -er. There is no limit except one that is set by one's own self.

"Argue for your limitations, and they are yours."
~Richard Bach

A couple of examples:

"Bill smoked marijuana for twenty years, and he is still extremely smart." But if Bill had not smoked marijuana for twenty years, he could have been a brain surgeon instead of a foot specialist, he could have been smart<u>er</u>, (Doesn't mean that he wanted to or meant to be a brain surgeon though).

Tim studies philosophy and watches "The Travel Channel", he is wise. But if Tim talked to many different types of people and actually traveled, he could be wis<u>er</u>.

~~~

War is the absence of love.

~~~

Possibly there is no point to this life, and by trying to find it, maybe one will only get stabbed by the point.

~~~

Even if this life has no point, it is still necessary to make it make sense, at least for the betterment of survival.

~~~

I wonder if people who use aphorisms are the most lost, or, are those who have raised themselves, and thus are self-guided.

~~~

Philosophy is about *not* accepting everything as the way it is: such as tradition and religion. It is instead about critically and crucially thinking outside of the boundaries to make better decisions for the utmost happiness, well-being, and survival of oneself and of humanity as a whole.

~~~

Philosophy teaches not what to think, but how to think. The why things are instead of the how things are. Philosophy explores why things exists, such as fire, instead of how they exist which is the job of science. Theoretical physicists study the Theory of Relativity, while philosophers study the relativity of theory.

~~~

It is not only language which separates us from the rest of the animal kingdom, it is more precisely creativity. Free will is found in creativity.

~~~

Sometimes we must get lost to find new ways. We must remember this next time we get lost, but remembering this while lost is nearly impossible.

~~~

If time is an illusion, then why do we get older? Saying that time is an illusion is only easy in the present moment.

~~~

Logic says that truth is exclusive, that something is *either* true or false, that it cannot be both. But truth is only exclusive in simple cases, such as whether a chair is green or not. But not in more complex cases such as personality. For example, just because someone is selfish at one time, does not mean that they are selfish all the time. They were simply selfish in a moment. A 'T' for 'true' cannot be branded on them for a factor of selfishness because of one act of selfishness. There is also much more to their personality than that. Also, just because a part of a car such as its bumper is broken, does not make it true that the car is broken as a whole. Truth and falsity are only exclusive is simple cases such as 'p and not p', not in more complex cases such as 'selfish' or 'broken'.

~~~

There are no self-evident truths.

~~~

To say that a rock is a rock is a tautology, but the message is still conveyed from person to person. It is the semantics, or meaning of the statement that is important, not the logical syntax. If someone tells me "An action is an action" (to use a different example), I know that person is negating the metaphysicalness of an action—he or she is wishing to be reserved on the subject and not engage in thinking to a deeper degree. The message would still be conveyed to me as it would to almost anyone else. Semantics are more human than syntax.

~~~

Life is only lived once no matter what one believes. In the case of Christianity, only one life is lived while on this Earth, then Heaven or Hell. Even in the case of reincarnation, only one life is lived during this particular life (there will be no memory of the other lives anyway). So this one life should be lived well, and it should not be waited until after this life is over to live it (oh, I'll just wait for Heaven where it'll be so much better, or oh, I'll just wait for the next life to fulfill myself). *There is only one chance regardless of beliefs.*

~~~

America is an empire, not by technical terms, but by motives and actions: vanity, materialism, blood lust, theatre, exploited sex, celebrities (which are the new genre of Greek Gods), having all of its resources spread out across the earth, having military bases secured around the world, spreading its beliefs and customs worldwide in order to slowly conquer all, and violently stopping any country who threatens its image, wealth, or resources. America is no different from empires such as Greece or Rome. These countries eventually fell due to their own gravity.

~~~

**Philosophy is the science-fiction of science.
Good science is always preceded by Philosophy, just
the same as science is always preceded by science-
fiction.**

~~~

**Humans are trapped between gods and animals. That
is what causes so must conflict of interest in this
world.**

~~~

**It is practically immeasurable how much one person
can affect another.**

~~~

**Philosophy comes to one like flashes of lightning. It
does not occur in a constant state.**

~~~

**Just because something is legal does not mean that
it is safe or healthy for you, and just because
something is illegal does not mean that it is not
healthy or safe for you.**

~~~

The universe is in a state of flux, but at different rates. Language is in motion slower than a fruit rots, and leaves turn brown slower than water runs. This must be taken into consideration when making temporal decisions regarding judgment and consequence.

~~~

My former take on ethics and morality was that they were simply rules imposed by society to keep the order of the deviant human animals. My new philosophy on morality and ethics is that we humans should try to expand and maximize what differentiates and distinguishes us from the rest of the animal kingdom, which is our cognition, our marked ability of self-awareness, and our detailed efficient, effective extremities. Following ethics and morality will help us better attain these goals by concentrating and focusing our learning into pathways that contain these ends by providing templates and structure.

~~~

"Ethical" should be about the maximization of consciousness for the affect of others, whether that be from psychedelics, prayer, or well-written books.

~~~

My ethical theory is as simple as this, one should always do good, as good is advantageous to the progress of life, and one should never do evil, as evil is inhibiting or disabling to the progress of life. This system also includes the fact that one only lives once, no matter what one believes (Heaven, Reincarnation, etc.), and that one should live to progress the life of oneself *and* others since they only live once as well. This progression of life also works in an interconnected way as progressing the life of one will in turn result in the progression of the life of others.

~~~

What would *you* do with the ring of Gyges (an invisibility ring from Plato's Republic)? Ask yourself this ultimate ethical question: If you had a ring that could make you invisible, and therefore you would face no consequences for any of your actions...what would you then do?

To bring it even further...what if there was no God to judge you either, a virtual world without consequence, what could then be your ultimate capacity for good or evil?

~~~

If you cannot prove it to be untrue, then you cannot claim it to be false (or vice-versa).

This is different in believing that something must be false just because you cannot prove it to be true, or that something must be true just because you cannot prove it to false (that would be the fallacious *argument from ignorance*). Instead, just because you cannot prove something to be true, doesn't mean that it is definitely false, but instead should remain open for debate or at least allowed the ability to exist for the mean time. The world was once thought with complete certainty to be flat because there was no proof which existed at the time that it was round, yet many people would have swore their lives to the death that the world was flat. The same holds true for those that claim there is no God. The God/souls debate cannot be proven to be either false or true, yet many claim that it is one way or the other. *The only people who truly know if there is a god are dead people*, and they don't speak, and even if they did, no one would believe it as fact 100% because doubts could always be raised about the nature of sanity, etc.

~~~

There is no specific answer to the meaning of life. There is no 'self' to be found. The only meaning and 'self' is one that is created, "Life is what you make it". It is up to the individual, not *anything* or *anyone* else. Believing in meaning to life such as fate can lead to a dependence on others for happiness, and believing in a fixed 'self' can lead to a resistance to change or adapting to the environment or circumstances. Spending time looking for meaning to why things happen such as love or death can also inhibit one's power to make correct decisions, by either wasting time or leading to hasty decisions. More comfort can be found in coincidence, randomness and circumstance for these reasons. For example, people just die. There is no need to spend time and energy thinking that someone died because that person was a bad person, or because of something that that person did, thus causing destruction of the mourner through fear and guilt. Randomness is clearly seen to play a role once the statistics are checked: millions of people die each year, millions are raped, millions are robbed—one is not alone. Things did not happen to only to one's self because of personal reasons. They are not alone. Checking the stats is the least one can do. Violence, drugs, and injustice have *always* been around since the beginning of history. Then again, maybe everything happens for a reason. Maybe every speck of dust in the universe is exactly where it is supposed to be. Maybe the past, present, and future exist simultaneously, and so everything is already planned out. But, regardless, searching for a fixed self or reasons for death can be a very dangerous slippery slope. These ideas are metaphysical, timeless, and unsolvable, but must be constantly weighed and considered. It is a lot of work, but sanity depends on it.

~~~

People often think that times are getting worse, "The future is bleak.", "There is more violence today than ever!", "People are doing drugs today more than ever!", these are commonly uttered through the crowds, but notice that *every* generation say the same things. When taken into historical perspective, human behavior remains relatively consistent. Violence, war, sex and drugs were even more prevalent and vicious in earlier times such as in the Greek and Roman days (orgies, slaves thrown to the lions, witches and witchcraft, public be-headings, impalements in the courtyards, etc.). If everything is looked at by a global, historical, or even cosmological level, then why things happen become much clearer and less destructive.

~~~

A meaning of life: realizations of love, forgiveness, peace, and interconnectedness.

~~~

Technology dehumanizes people by cutting off the connections between relations with other people and nature, (e.g., social gatherings, fishing, hunting, camping, gardening, communicating in person), while it simultaneously enlightens what is *most* human, that is providing maximum ability to systematize and process information beyond what could be accomplished before, increasing the full potential of our distinct, marked cognition.

~~~

Sometimes "higher" technology is not better than the previous "lower" technology.

~~~

Technology introduces new categories of thought. A good example is that at one time no category for mass agriculture existed. Categories such as radio waves, mobile phones, laptops, and electronic machines also introduced new categories, amongst countless others.

~~~

Feelings/emotions are inconsistent, they can change by the second and are largely to be ignored in intellectual conversations, but these feelings are still a large part of what makes us human. Feelings are still hurt, rage can still sometimes be necessary, and euphoria serves a purpose.

~~~

There seems to be an increasing deterioration in the amount of time there is for reflection—the more possessions (abstract, concrete, technological, etc.), the more need there is to maintain and progress these possessions according to personal and societal standards.

~~~

The maintenance of possessions is brutal.

~~~

Truth is something considered *by most* to be something which can be understood by an entire population at once. Though absolute truth is objective, it is many times subject to whole populations that agree on certain principles which are only *deemed* as true, since objectivity is never fully certain through the interpretations of humans. This is so because we are having subjective experiences of objective reality.

~~~

It is possible for many to acquire too much knowledge.

Only so much can be digested at a time. For a humorous example, imagine walking into the Library and having all of its information absorbed into your brain simultaneously. For a serious example, imagine gaining the knowledge of how it feels to murder, be murdered, raped, tortured, or all of the above. This is knowledge that few could handle well, if at all. All this being said, one has to make a decision on how much knowledge one wants to ingest and absorb. It is a personal decision, a personal setting of limitations. Some want to know it all regardless of consequence, some want to know as little as possible, also regardless of consequence. Settings of personal mental limitations is personal, and should be respected, and tolerated. This is a right.

~~~

All anyone wants is 'Being'...no matter what it takes, or does not take. But, don't just 'be', but 'be' something. It takes a lot of work to 'be' just as it does not to 'be'. Homeostasis takes maintenance.

~~~

Anything can be rationalized through elaborate combinations of personal philosophies.

~~~

If all stimuli affects behavior, then does free-will exist?
Free will only exists through a small of amount of thought involved in pure creativity. Examples are Einstein's theory of relativity, Heidegger's book *Being and Time*, and Picasso's cubism. These may not be purely novel creations, borrowed bits and pieces from elsewhere, but novelty does arise, and does so through creative thought. Proof of this is in never before seen creations of all kinds, from bridges to statues to paintings to stories. This may only happen once every hundred years, but it still happens.

~~~

Instead of considering myself as a smart-ass, I consider myself as a dumb-ass to give myself room to move and grow.

~~~

You will graduate a Philosophy program knowing less than when you started. This is a good thing, questioning everything, and not taking all stimuli and information as ultimate truth, on first given face value. There is more than our senses can offer. This is important to never become ensnared or enslaved by one's self or surroundings.

~~~

There is no worse personality than a mister know-it-all. He or she cannot be convinced of anything different, and so usually tries to control and cement facts into being. This leads to blockage and stoppage of others exploring their bodies, minds, and environments.

~~~

There is a constant struggle in academia between knowing and not knowing, i.e., between acquiring knowledge and knowing that that knowledge is limited and should only be taken as a 'grain of salt'. Once knowledge is obtained, it can be used or transmitted in some way to others. But, it is hard to transmit that that knowledge is not the all and end all. People usually do not listen if they think you are unsure about what you attempt to profess to be true. It is simply the best we've got at the time, including all forms of science and mathematics—the world was once believed to be flat! "Facts are stubborn", but how else are we supposed to ever teach and contribute to the world of ideas?, except by realizing that "Facts are flexible". "There are no facts, only interpretations."   -Nietzsche

~~~

The experience of God, is basically that since birth, the unconscious collects and stores information that one recognizes. It becomes a deep and vast library for that person; it becomes wiser than that person in comparison to their shallow consciousness. Besides for dreams or drugs, prayer and meditation are seemingly the only way to access the unconsciousness. When one prays, one is accessing a personal library, communicating and maximizing his or her brain by simultaneously reaching it at all levels (from the unconsciousness to the consciousness). The maximization of the brain is what causes a feeling of euphoria since the brain is human beings' greatest asset and for us possesses the most power. That person may also confuse receiving information from their personal library as being from an outside source, such as a God, feeling comforted by thinking that they are reassured in not being alone, and by having gained 'wisdom' from their 'helper'. It is irrelevant that one's personal library or memory is not dependable, insufficient, and fallacious--as long as someone *believes* that the memories are 'real' it will most often go unquestioned and still lead to a belief in communication with God.

But just because God may arise from unconscious processes, does not mean that that same God is not a part of the external, because the outside contains the inside, and the inside contains the outside. All is one, all is dependant upon everything else, and so what is in you is also without you. So God is All, both in your head and outside your skull. The reason is because the two are connected, since all is interconnected and One.

~~~

My mediation method is as simple as this - 2 minutes, at least twice a day, to just be in the present moment *completely.* No worries about the past or future, to just hear the birds sing as music. Most of the time when we hear birds sing or cars pass, or any other everyday noise, our ego-active minds distinguish: that is a bird, that is a car, that is a squirrel, etc., etc. Stop naming, stop categorizing, for a moment. Just hear the noise and sounds around you as music, as music of being a part of, and on the Earth, manifestations of the Universe. Just experience things and movements as they are and are happening, do not think about what they are and what they are doing. To just be completely and absolutely present, for at least 2 minutes, twice a day. When you can, spend more time there. This is my meditation method.

~~~

I aim to never be categorized. I want to be free from all ways of being placed into 'molds' of some form or another. I want to break free from all 'molds'. But, there is a point where the boundaries must stay to allow me to co-exist with other people.

~~~

There is no such thing as a perfect argument that holes cannot be shot through by someone or something at one point or another.

~~~

The ultimate goal of the Philosophy of Perception is to describe the way the world is apart from perceiving minds, or to study the nature of perception in objective means. But this is impossible, since we cannot escape the bounds of human perception in the first place in order to study how we are ultimately perceiving. *There exists the boundary between the inside of our skulls and the world which may or may not surround it.*

~~~

'Consciousness' is a system, like digestion, which is comprised of components. When one of the components is affected, then all of the components are affected. For example, if memory is affected, then the rest of consciousness is affected, such as in the case of Alzheimer's or amnesia. If the pre-frontal cortex is affected, then mood or personality can be affected, such as in the case of Phineas Gage. *Alter the brain, alter the mind.* Take 5 shots of tequila, and watch how your consciousness is altered. But, it is also possible that consciousness is like a receiver, sort of like a television antennae, that receives information from the Universe. When the antennae is altered or damaged, such as in the case of taking five shots of tequila, then the reception become blunted and blurred, cutting off consciousness from cosmic energy, causing the individual to become less conscious.

Whatever it is..., 'consciousness' is *the* most powerful aspect of humanity.

~~~

Live as though you are already old looking back on your life.

www.ingramcontent.com/pod-product-compliance
Lightning Source LLC
Chambersburg PA
CBHW060640290526
45793CB00001B/327